Timeline of My Family History

Nancy Anderson

Rosen REAL READERS

Rosen Classroom™
New York

My grandmother is helping me with a school project. She is helping me make a timeline of my family history. She tells me about her parents.

My grandmother's parents are my great-grandparents. They were born in Italy in 1920. They got married in Italy, too.

My great-grandparents moved to the United States in 1945. They came to the United States through Ellis Island.

My great-grandparents settled in New York. They opened a bakery. The bakery is still there today. My mom and dad own it.

In 1950, my great-grandparents had their first child. They had a baby girl. She would later become my grandmother.

My grandfather fought in the Vietnam War. He came back from the war in 1969. He met my grandmother when he got back. They got married in 1974.

My grandmother had a baby boy in 1976. He is my dad. My dad helped out at my great-grandparents' bakery as a child.

My mom and dad met each other in 1996. They got married in 2001.

I was born in 2006. I write this on my timeline. I put photographs on my timeline, and I color it, too.

1920	My great-grandparents are born.	
1945	My great-grandparents move to the United States.	
1950	My grandmother is born.	
1974	My grandparents get married.	
1976	My dad is born.	
2001	My mom and dad get married.	
2006	I am born.	

Here is my timeline. I learned a lot about my family by making this timeline. It is fun learning about my family history!

Words to Know

bakery

Ellis Island

grandmother

great-grandparents

timeline

Vietnam War